Published by Arcadia Children's Books
A Division of Arcadia Publishing
Charleston, SC
www.arcadiapublishing.com

Copyright © 2021 by Arcadia Children's Books • All rights reserved
First published 2021 • Manufactured in the United States
ISBN 978-1-4671-9813-4

Library of Congress Control Number: 2021932666

All images used © Shutterstock.com, pp. 6-7 DavidJM / Shutterstock.
com; p. 9 Matthew Dicker / Shutterstock.com; p. 21 Eliyahu Yosef
Parypa / Shutterstock.com; p. 28 T Esq / Shutterstock.com; p. 37
EarthScape ImageGraphy / Shutterstock.com; p. 40 Victoria Lipov /
Shutterstock.com; p. 41 Christopher Penler / Shutterstock.com; pp.
42, 63 (top) S-F / Shutterstock.com; p. 50 1000 Words / Shutterstock.
com; p. 53 lev radin / Shutterstock.com; p. 55 Osugi / Shutterstock.
com; pp. 58-59 DW labs Incorporated / Shutterstock.com; p. 60
photravel_ru / Shutterstock.com; p. 62 Mia2you / Shutterstock.
com; p. 63 (bottom) littlenySTOCK / Shutterstock.com; p. 67
ruigsantos / Shutterstock.com; pp. 76-77 Joseph Sohm / Shutterstock.
com; p. 78 Debby Wong / Shutterstock.com; p. 90 Amy Corti /
Shutterstock.com; p. 92-93 Alessio Catelli / Shutterstock.com.

Craig Yoe has written a TON of kids'
joke books! Yoe has been a creative
director for Nickelodeon, Disney, and
Jim Henson at the Muppets. Raised
in the Midwest, he has lived from
New York to California and has six kids!

Cover illustration: Craig Yoe
Cover design: David Hastings
Page design: Jessica Nevins

CONTENTS

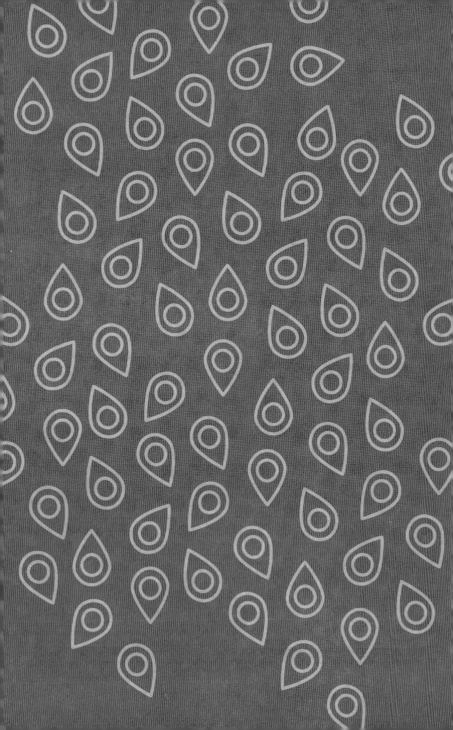

SMART FACTOID

The NYPL has over 50 million books—lots of stories to read!

KNOCK! KNOCK!

WHO'S THERE?
Strand.

STRAND WHO?
Strand-in' right here, waiting for our book club meeting!

BOOKISH FACTOID:

The Strand Bookstore has over 18 miles of bookshelves! Wow!

The Strand Bookstore

BiGFOOT FACTOiD: Lady Liberty wears a size 879 shoe!

Why does the Statue of Liberty stand in New York Harbor?

Because she can't sit down!

COLOR BLIND FACTOID

Cabs in NYC weren't originally yellow. They were red and green!

Why can't a man living in New York City be buried in Los Angeles?

Because he's not dead!

EXPENSIVE FACTOID

It would cost **$19,000** to take a taxi from NYC to LA!

Which New York City neighborhoods have the best sense of humor?

Har-Harlem and SoHo-Ho!

What did the witch order at the New York Hilton?

Broom service!

When a US Airways passenger plane landed in the Hudson River in 2009, Circle Line sightseeing boats were among the first to come to the rescue! (And everyone was rescued safely.)

Roar!

What goes round and roars?

The Circle Lion Tour!

Why was the skater at Rockefeller Plaza feeling full?

He 8 a lot!

Where did the young pine tree learn to become the Rockefeller Plaza Christmas tree?

In Elemen-TREE school!

Rockefeller Plaza

What is the shape of the Rockefeller Plaza Christmas tree?

A **TREE**-angle!

BRiGHT FACTOiD

Bright Factoid: The Christmas tree in Rockefeller Plaza glows with over 50,000 LED lights!

CULTURAL FACTOID

Over 100 sculptures,
murals, and mosaics by 39
different artists decorate
Rockefeller Center!

Where's the happiest place in the Big Apple?

The New-York **HYSTERICAL** Society!

HISTORICAL FACTOID:

The fun and fascinating New-York Historical Society was New York's first museum, founded in 1804!

New York cop: Why did you park here?

Tourist: The sign says, "Fine for parking!"

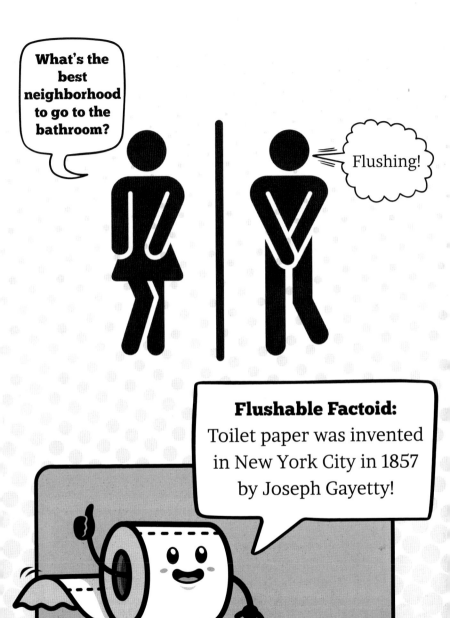

ELECTRIC FACTOID

The Empire State Building gets struck by lightning about 25 times per year!

What can you get in the Waldorf Astoria hotel?

SUITE dreams!

In what part of Manhattan do kids practice the multiplication tables?

Times Square!

If a six-foot man jumps into the East River in a red swim suit at noon, what does he get?

Wet!

FUN FACTOID

The East River is not a river, it's technically a tidal estuary. (What's that? I don't know. Look it up!)

FAST FACTOID

The New York City Transit Authority operates the world's largest fleet of buses: 4,373 public buses, serving more than 665 million people a year!

Which NYC transportation is the crabbiest?

The **CROSS**town bus!

CAN YOU GIVE ME DIRECTIONS, PLEASE?

New York City has Uptown, Downtown,
the East Side, and the West Side*!
Now that you know that, let the jokes begin!

(*It also has a Midtown, a Lower East Side,
an Upper East Side, an Upper West Side,
but **NOT** a Lower West Side . . .)

**What's a goose's
favorite part of town?**

DOWNtown!

**Where are the best
bakeries in the
Big Apple?**

The
YEAST
side!

WHO'S THERE?
Sup'?

SUP' WHO?
Sup' Town!

Where's the best place for a selfie?

The **BEST** side!

HISTORICAL FACTOID

The first female subway conductor was hired in 1917!

If laid end-to-end, the Big Apple's subway tracks would stretch from New York City to Chicago!

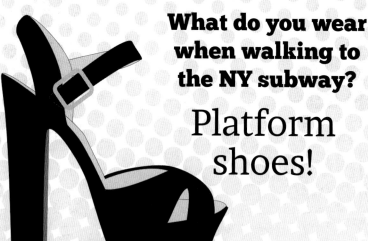

How do you know that a subway just went by?

You can see the tracks!

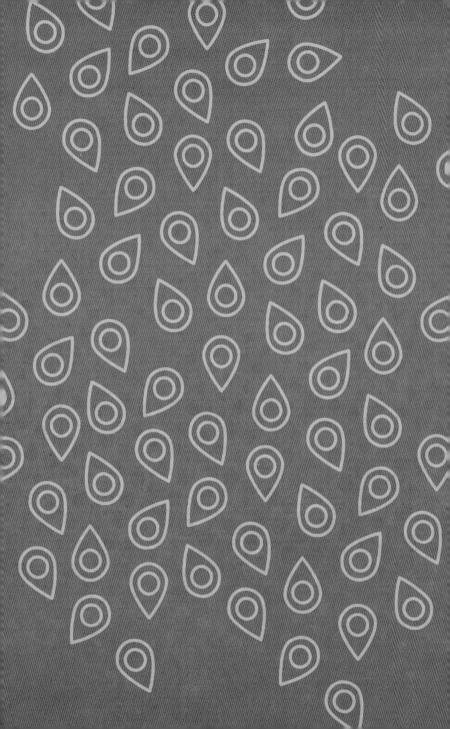

WHERE'S the best place to meet a star?

FiVE POiNTS!

HISTORICAL FACTOID:

Five Points was a neighborhood near today's Chinatown.
(It was a pretty rough place back in the late 1860s, controlled by rival gangs!)

WHERE can you get your wishes granted in New York?

The Staten Island **FAIRY**!

Staten Island Ferry

WHERE'S the best place to charge your phone?

BATTERY Park City!

WHERE'S the best place in the Big Apple to get vegetables?

In Madison **SQUASH** Garden!

Madison Square Garden

44

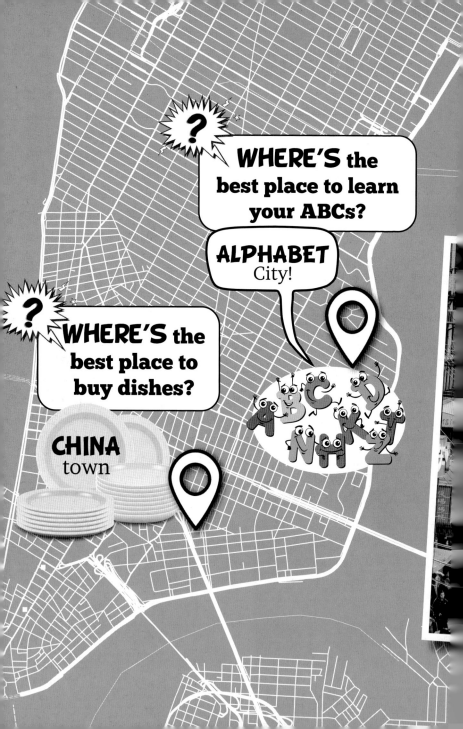

INTERNATIONAL FACTOID:

The Big Apple has the largest Chinese population of any city outside of Asia!

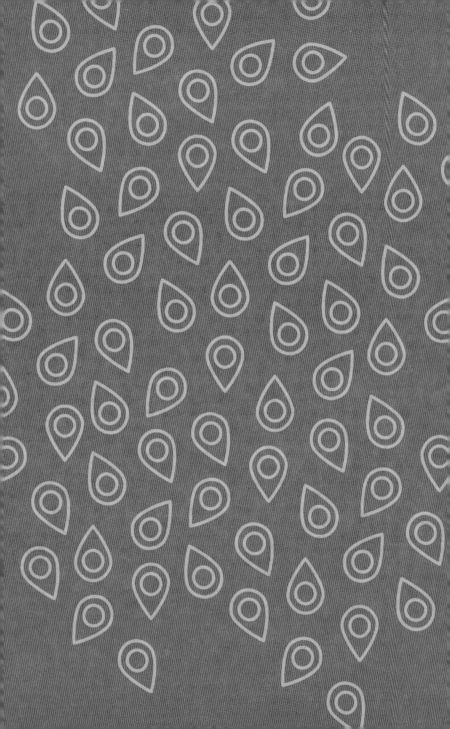

The Museum of Modern Art

AT THE MUSEUM OF MODERN ART:

Tourist: Can we take pictures?

Guard: No, the paintings have to stay on the walls!

What did the Greenwich Village art gallery say when it was lonely?

I want my **MOMA**!

WEIRD BUT TRUE FACTOID:
One of the now priceless works of art in the MoMA collection is a fur-covered teacup the museum director bought in 1936 (for $50)!

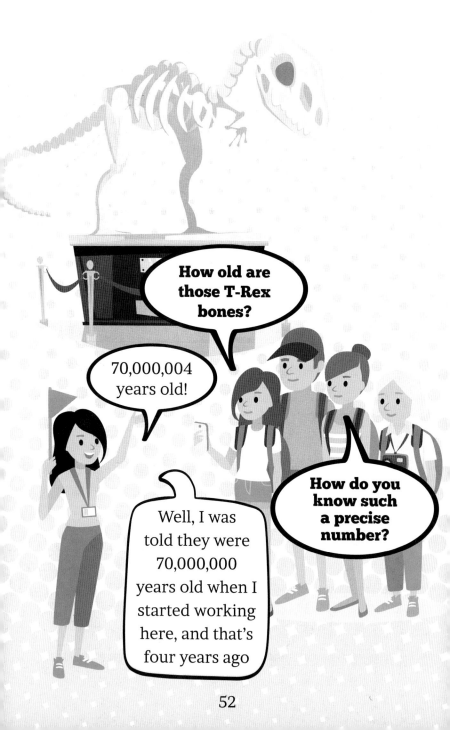

Which New York City attraction will put you over the moon?

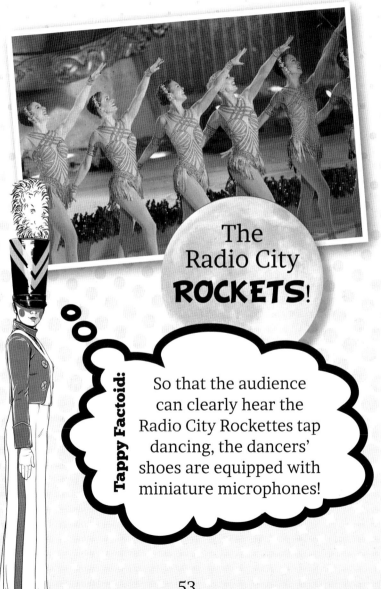

The
Radio City
ROCKETS!

Tappy Factoid: So that the audience can clearly hear the Radio City Rockettes tap dancing, the dancers' shoes are equipped with miniature microphones!

Where does a librarian from the Morgan Library sleep?

Between the covers!

MONSTROUS FACTOID:

The Morgan Library has Mary Shelley's original manuscript of Frankenstein.

A photon walks into the Plaza Hotel.

The desk clerk says, "Can we help you with your luggage?"

The photon says, "No, thanks. I'm traveling light."

WORD UP! The Plaza Hotel is where the famed children's book *Eloise* takes place.

The Plaza Hotel

What do you get if you combine the Museum of Modern Art and Sarge's Delicatessen?

Where are people the friendliest in the Big Apple?

On the **"HI!"** Line!

GOBBLE GOBBLE FACTOID:

The last train to run on the elevated tracks that are now the popular High Line came through in 1980 and carried three cars loaded with frozen turkeys!

Tenement Museum

HISTORICAL FACTOID:

The Tenement Museum explores the American story of immigration and is housed in what was a once falling-down tenement building that had been empty for more than fifty years.

What do you do when you go to the entrance of the New York Public Library?

You cross the lions!

Why did Dracula go to the New York Public Library?

He wanted to sink his teeth into a good book!

How do books at the New York Public Library go to bed?

They snuggle under the covers.

Why did the yogurt go to the Metropolitan Museum of Art?

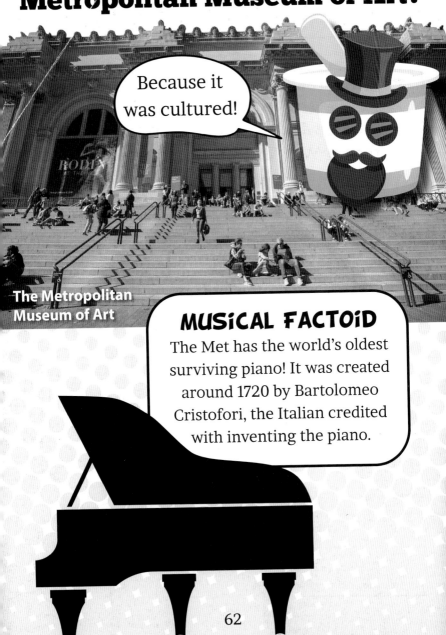

Because it was cultured!

The Metropolitan Museum of Art

MUSICAL FACTOID
The Met has the world's oldest surviving piano! It was created around 1720 by Bartolomeo Cristofori, the Italian credited with inventing the piano.

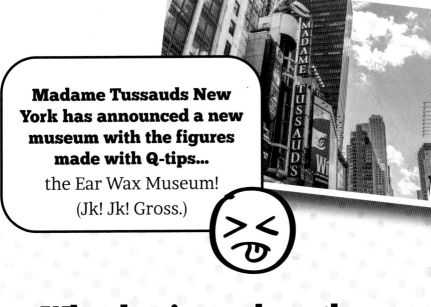

Madame Tussauds New York has announced a new museum with the figures made with Q-tips...
the Ear Wax Museum! (Jk! Jk! Gross.)

Why do pirates love the New York City Opera?

Because they love the high Cs!

Lincoln Center

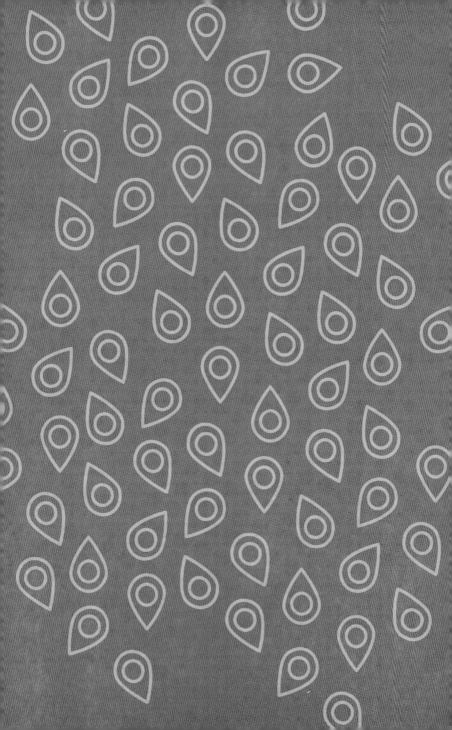

Where did the cow go for an exciting vacation?

MOO York City!

MOO-tastic Factoid:
The United States' first cattle ranch was started on New York's Long Island in 1747!

Which dog is the most popular in the Big Apple?

A New **YORK-IE!**

Arf! Arf!

CANINE FACTOID

More than 600,000 dogs live in New York City!

What's worse than raining cats and dogs?

Hailing New York City taxis!

Where do over eight million salamanders live?

In **NEWT** York City!

Where does Peppa Pig play in New York City?

Central **PORK**!

Film Factoid:

The most filmed public park on the planet, Central Park, has played a role in nearly 250 major movies!

Central Park

Lemur at the Bronx Zoo

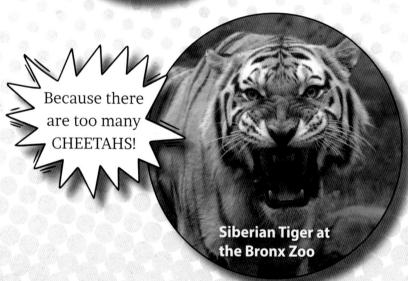

Siberian Tiger at the Bronx Zoo

FROGGY FACTOID:

The Bronx Zoo saved Tanzania's Kihansi spray toad, a species of toad that had been declared extinct!

Tanzania's Kihansi spray toad

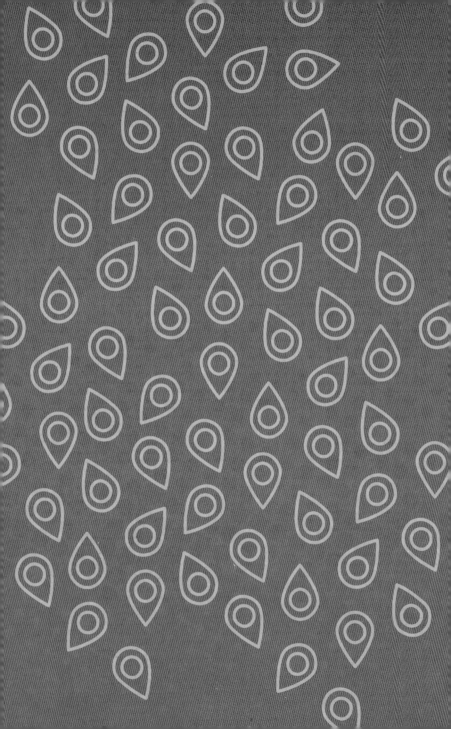

Why is Yankee Stadium the world's coolest place to go?

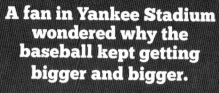

A fan in Yankee Stadium wondered why the baseball kept getting bigger and bigger.

Then it HIT him!

Safe! Factoid:
The home of the New York Yankees was the first ballpark to be called a stadium!

Yankee Stadium

Which New York Mets baseball player makes pancakes?

The batter!

HEE-HAW FACTOID:

The NY Mets' mascot was once a mule!

What has 18 legs and catches flies?

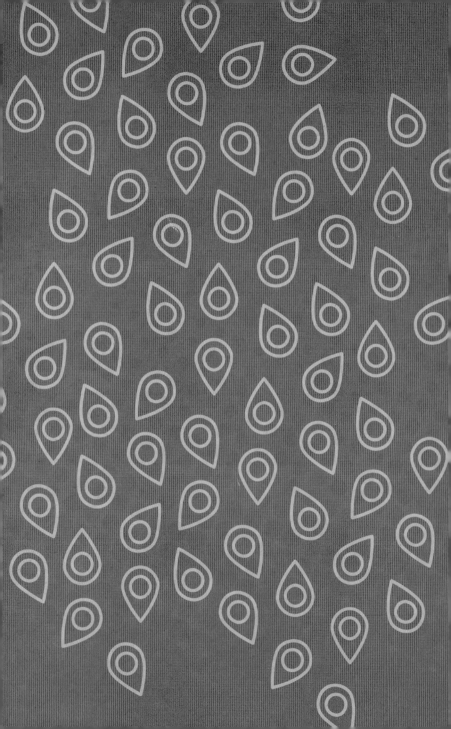

Did you hear the joke about New York pizza?

Never mind, it's too cheesy!

DELICIOUS FACTOID:

New Yorkers are famous for folding their pizza slices in half so they can eat them on the go, yo!

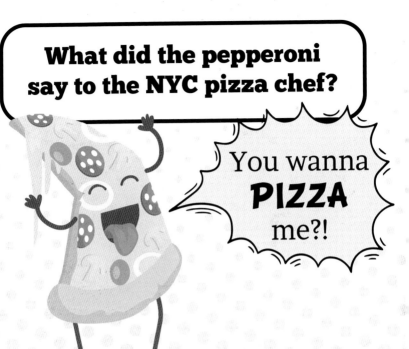

What did the pepperoni say to the NYC pizza chef?

You wanna **PIZZA** me?!

Fugetaboutit Factoid:
The Pizza Hall of Fame recognizes Lombardi's Pizza in Little Italy as the first pizzeria in the United States. It opened in 1905!

What do you do when you eat a Nathan's hot dog?

Relish the moment!

SOOOO MANY HOT DOGS FACTOID:

The record for the most hot dogs eaten in 10 minutes is **75**! That record was set in 2020 at the Nathan's Famous International Hot Dog Eating Contest, which is held every Fourth of July in Coney Island.

What do you call it when a kitten walks into Katz's Deli?

A Deli-CAT situation!

Delicious Factoid:

Katz's Delicatessen, founded in 1888, is the oldest Jewish deli on Earth and home of the planet's best pastrami*!

*This is the author's opinion, and he's eaten a lot of pastrami! Do you have a favorite?

Where did the tourist from India eat in New York?

At the **NEW DELI**!

Hey, you never showed up for dinner in Little Italy!

Sorry I didn't see you—I walked right **PASTA**!

Welcome to *Little Italy*

Little Italy

90

A lady walks into the New York Public Library and says, "I'll have a hot dog wit mustard and relish!" The librarian says, "Excuse me, ma'am, do you know this is a library?" So the lady says, "Oh, sorry!" and then WHISPERS, "I'll have a hot dog wit mustard and relish."

DELICIOUS FACTOID

The ice-cream cone was invented in New York City!

Where's the best place in New Yawk to get ice cream?

CONE-y
Island

Coney Island

How do you make a New York hot dog stand?

Sing the National Anthem!

Award-Winning Factoid:
New York food stands and trucks have their own awards! The Vendy Awards give honors to the Big Apple's best street food vendors! Yum!

NEW YORKERS

LOX AND BAGELS!
Dept.

LOX is smoked salmon and the perfect topping for a New Yorker's bodacious bagel!

What do tourists want with their bagels, you ask?

A locksmith from Luxembourg gets LOCKS and bagels!

A Facebook fan from France gets LIKES and bagels!

A model from Monaco gets LOOKS and bagels!

A plumber from Peru get LEAKS and bagels!

An ice-cream maker from Iceland gets LICKS and bagels!

95

However, what kind of bagel do the pilots who fly these tourists to the Big Apple want?!

PLANE bagels!

BAGEL-Y FACTOID:

A bagel is the only bread that is boiled before it's baked (which gives it its chewy, crusty goodness)! *

*And New York is famous for them!